Little CAB Press

I0189873

Weeds in the Flower Pot

Dianna Beamis Good

Little CAB
Press

Weeds in the Flower Pot By Dianna Beamis Good
Cover Art by Gretchen White

Published by Little CAB Press

www.littlecabpress.com

Published in the United States of America

ISBN: 978-0692950777

Dedicated to
my husband, David,
who is blind to my weeds
and only <u>sees</u> the flower

Acknowledgements

Thank you to my Lord God who saved this wicked sinner and set her free.

Thank you, my David, for your unwavering patience and love.

To my mom, children and beautiful grandchildren, you are my heart.

Thank you, Alice Klies, for your never failing encouragement every time I wanted to set this aside. You are my lifeline.

Thank you, Sharon Chase, for your patience dear friend.

Thank you, Dad, I'll be seeing you in Heaven one day.

To those who read my ramblings, know that these are from the mind of someone, I pray, you loved and who loved you deeply in return. These free-floating thoughts are real, nothing manufactured or designed. This is evident in the sometimes twists and turns. You are a part of me that makes me the happiest I will ever be. Only you could have done this with your unconditional love and acceptance of all my flaws. I pray for love, happiness and contentment.

Weeds in the Flower Pot is a book about life, everyone's life. I am no expert on other's thoughts, but I do believe we all share in the same insecurities, doubt, loneliness, hope, love, compassion and a need for connections.

I would love for us to be able to break the shackles of silence, scream to the tallest mountain that we are human and we make mistakes and it's okay.

We should not be ashamed. I was told once by a very wise man, "You know, Dianna, there was only one perfect person that ever walked this Earth, and it wasn't you". Jesus Christ is our perfect example that we should try our best to imitate, but sometimes we just mess up.

I'm no Bible scholar, yet I know the Bible is filled with encouraging words of forgiveness and God's understanding of our failures. In fact, he tells us not if we fail, but when we fail, He will be with us with a heart full of love. God throws our messes as far as the east is from the west.

God also says we will have trials and tribulations—translation—we will have weeds grow, die, and grow again in our beautiful flower-filled pot in our lives.

If we know all this and the Bible is quite clear about it, then why are we so reluctant to talk about our shortcomings and frustrations with this beautiful life God has given us? Is it perfect? No, thus the weeds. Is there beauty is this world? Yes, thus the flower pot.

I want us, through these pages of often random thoughts, to tackle the hard issues of life head on. You may read a page and say "huh?" and that's okay. Read it again and think through the words again for what they may be saying about your life. Discuss it with a friend over coffee and see what they discovered. You may learn something that will amaze you and possibly comfort you.

Weeds in the Flower Pot was assembled from my journal of thoughts about life, family, aging and who I really am and what I am becoming. After sharing a few thoughts to a couple of friends, I realized I wasn't alone with my weeds. My friends had a few of their own. So perhaps you can weed your beautiful pot with a friend or two, your spouse or a group of friends and see what you discover.

I pray these honest and raw feelings give you permission to write about your weeds and dig deeper for a closer understanding of yourself or someone you love and above all bring you nearer to the Heart of our Savior.

So grab your garden gloves and let's start digging.

Scriptures are from the English Standard version

Table of Contents

After Church One Sunday

I am an alien floating in my multi-colored bubble on my own planet. I'm surrounded by those who seem to be the perfect "Stepford" wives. Put together with effortless grace. A Bible verse on the tip of their tongue, fit for any occasion. The thoughts and motives of their hearts appear always pure. A negative or sinful idea, I'm sure, never enters their minds. I don't dare speak a word in fear they may discover that I am not one of them and they will banish me as sinful and unworthy. What would happen if I open up to them about my struggles in reading the Bible every morning or how my thoughts stray? Maybe I would find out I'm not alone.

Romans 3:23 "For all have sinned and fall short of the glory of God."

Galatians 3:28 "There is neither Jew nor Greek, there is neither slave nor free, there is no male or female, for you are all one in Christ Jesus."

_____

_____

_____

_____

_____

_____

_____

_____

_____

An Anxious Day

My heart races. The knot in my stomach grows tighter and tighter. The wanting, the anticipation. The minutes are like hours. The "watched pot never boils." Lord, I need you now. I need your comfort and sense of peace. I know you're here, even if I don't feel it. The shackles of pain and depression are wrapped closely around my mind. Like a boa constrictor, it starts to squeeze. I see peace and contentment just out of reach with its arms spread wide, beckoning me to come closer. I look more closely at the pain, I realize it doesn't hold me. I hold onto it. All I have to do is open my hand. Why do I trap myself with my own mind? It's time to let go for good.

Philippians 4:8-9 "Finally, brothers, whatever is true, whatever is honorable, whatever is just, whatever is pure, whatever is lovely, whatever is commendable, if there is any excellence, if there is anything worthy of praise, think about these things. What you have learned and received and heard and seen in me—practice these things, and the God of peace will be with you.

"A time to seek, and a time to lose; a time to keep, and a time to cast away"

_____

_____

_____

_____

_____

_____

_____

_____

_____

_____

~ 3 ~
I'm How Old?

The clocks tick throughout the house. They seem to increases in volume. I am at first only mildly annoyed by this intrusion. However, as the sound continues, my tension grows. I run to each room. I pluck the clocks off their perch one by one and toss them in the trash. The realization of life without the constraints of time fills me with a sense of unimaginable freedom. Why is it I allow time to map my days. I am given orders to go here, then there? Why have I allowed time to dictate when I am old and when it may be time to die?

Psalm 46:10 "Be still, and know that I am God. I will be exalted among the nations, I will be exalted in the earth!"

Romans 8:28 "And we know that for those who love God all things work together for good, for those who are called according to his purpose."

_____

_____

_____

_____

_____

_____

_____

_____

_____

_____

~ 4 ~
The Look of Love

We can love so deeply. But in that cavernous pool, so often an unwanted speck of dust may cause a tiny ripple. The love remains, but its usual calm state is disturbed. If the speck is left on its own, it will fall to the depths of the pool. The mind may keep it ever present and even allow a variety of particles to settle. Suddenly the once pure pool has become muddied and polluted. It's rarely a heap of debris that mars the glassy pool, but the small specks that over time changes the look of love.

I John 3:1 "See what kind of love the Father has given to us, that we should be called children of God; and so we are. The reason why the world does not know us is that it did not know him."

I Peter 3:8 "Finally, all of you, have unity of mind, sympathy, brotherly love, a tender heart, and a humble mind."

_____

_____

_____

_____

_____

_____

_____

_____

_____

~ 5 ~
Why Don't I Reach Out?

The smallest thing: a phone call, card sent and received, smile, hello, "How are you?" said with sincerity can send my spirits soaring. How long would it take to help someone else be blessed? How much of my day would be spent? The rewards are immeasurable, and it's such a small thing. Why don't I do it more often?

1 John 4:11 "Beloved, if God so loved us, we also ought to love one another"

Romans 13:10 "Love does no wrong to a neighbor; therefore love is the fulfilling of the law."

_____

_____

_____

_____

_____

_____

_____

_____

_____

_____

_____

~ 6 ~
I Feel Nothing

The mind is closed. Nothing new can drill through the emotional cement wall the brain built. A word or idea may attempt to scale it, but it falls unsuccessful. The wall seems almost impenetrable, but I try to focus and I observe a small gap. The smallest ray of light dimly seeps through. I concentrate on this beam of hope that may break down the wall of sadness, anxiety and pain. The light of God's goodness, mercy and grace can break down any wall. I must let it happen. A piece falls. As I continue to focus on this one, others may come down brick by brick.

Isaiah 41:10 "Fear not, for I am with you; be not dismayed, for I am your God; I will strengthen you, I will help you, I will uphold you with my righteous right hand."

Matthew 11:28-30 "Come to me, all who labor and are heavy laden, and I will give you rest. Take my yoke upon you, and learn from me, for I am gentle and lowly in heart, and you will find rest for your souls. For my yoke is easy, and my burden is light."

_____

_____

_____

_____

_____

_____

_____

_____

_____

~ 7 ~
A New Day

As the alarm awakens your mind to the new day, do you groan and glare at it with dread? Or do you leisurely roll over and smile at the world with hopeful anticipation? How do you want to start each day?

Lamentations 3:22-23 "The steadfast love of the Lord never ceases; his mercies never come to an end; they are new every morning; great is your faithfulness."

Jeremiah 29:11-12 "For I know the plans I have for you, declares the Lord, plans for welfare and not for evil, to give you a future and a hope. Then you will call upon me and come and pray to me, and I will hear you."

_____

_____

_____

_____

_____

_____

_____

_____

_____

_____

~ 8 ~
Are You There, God?

God, it's so dark and cold in here. Do you see me? Can you hear me? Anyone else up there? I feel only sadness and despair surrounding me. Anyone there? God help! But wait, you've been here before. "Let this cup pass from me," you said. But it didn't, did it? You've felt what I feel. You know this pit. Wait, I see a light. Is that you, God?

John 1:14 "And the Word became flesh and dwelt among us, and we have seen his glory, glory as of the only Son from the Father, full of grace and truth."

I Corinthians 10:13 "No temptation has overtaken you that is not common to man. God is faithful, and he will not let you be tempted beyond your ability, but with the temptation he will also provide the way of escape, that you may be able to endure it."

_____

_____

_____

_____

_____

_____

_____

_____

_____

_____

~ 9 ~
Grow Up?

Maybe it's time to get my head out of the clouds and act my age. The problem is, I don't know how my age is supposed to act? Does it mean stop riding the grocery carts to my car, or stop dancing in the rain or even give up swinging on a playground? What does it actually mean to act my age? It means I start to give up who I am inside and act as others think I should.

II Corinthians 3:17 "Now the Lord is the Spirit, and where the Spirit of the Lord is, there is freedom."

John 8:32 "And you will know the truth, and the truth will set you free,"

_____

_____

_____

_____

_____

_____

_____

_____

_____

_____

_____

~ 10 ~
What is Love?

Love is not a feeling. It is a commitment from one person to another. Our heart and soul are part of someone who shares our hopes and dreams. Too many people base it on how it feels. Feelings deceive and often trick us into false hope and desire. True love is not hearts and roses, but it's a shared life with another who dreams the same dream.

I Corinthians 13:4-7 "Love is patient and kind; love does not envy or boast; it is not arrogant or rude. It does not insist on its own way; it is not irritable or resentful; it does not rejoice at wrongdoing, but rejoices with the truth. Love bears all things, believes all things, hopes all things, endures all things."

_____

_____

_____

_____

_____

_____

_____

_____

_____

_____

We Are Not Alone

I crawl through the flames and shadows fall around me. The gunshots ring and mortar deaden my senses. Smoke crowds my lungs for air. A bullet paralyzes my movement and my body crumbles to the ground. The enemy advances. I quake with fear. A figure appears in the haze, but I can't see. The back of my hand wipes away the dust and grime from my eyes. I cry out. He turns, walks back and lifts me to safety while shots miraculously pass us by.

After he lays me gently on the ground I ask, "Who are you?"

He merely replies, "I have always been and will always be. I am the Alpha, Omega, the beginning and the end. I will carry you through to eternity."

Isaiah 41:10 "Fear not, for I am with you; be not dismayed, for I am your God; I will strengthen you, I will help you, I will uphold you with my righteous right hand."

Psalm 139:7-10 "Where shall I go from your Spirit? Or where shall I flee from your presence? If I ascend to heaven, you are there! If I make my bed in Sheol, you are there! If I take the wings of the morning and dwell in the uttermost parts of the sea, even there your hand shall lead me, and your right hand shall hold me."

_____

_____

_____

_____

_____

_____

_____

_____

~ 12 ~
Pushing Through

The start of a new day. Lost in dreams of what could be. Something wakes me—a dog barks, a bird chirps. As my mind wakes, all is perfect with the world, but the moment only last a fraction of a second when the trap door shuts me outside of Eden. The feeling comes back in a titanic wave of despair. It washes over my body from head to toe. A physical ache. The loneliness, the knot in the stomach, the fear. But as I have every other day with all I possess, I willfully push my way out of the pit to start a new day. God is good.

Matthew 5:16 "In the same way, let your light shine before others, so that they may see your good works and give glory to your Father who is in heaven."

Hebrews 4:12 "For the word of God is living and active, sharper than any two-edged sword, piercing to the division of soul and of spirit, of joints and of marrow, and discerning the thoughts and intentions of the heart."

_____

_____

_____

_____

_____

_____

_____

_____

_____

_____

My Reflection

Where did it go? How did I get here? I look in the mirror each morning and see my image, but I'm always taken aback, just for a split second. My eyes once again are surprised by the subtle signs of age that my mind doesn't seem to recognize. The small lines around the eyes. The slight droop around the lips where gravity takes over. I don't feel older, yet if I am completely honest, I do. My workouts take longer. My joints scream once I sit down. The tiredness settles in around 9 p.m. and, of course, the muscle groans each morning. Is this what it means to age? The body betrays. The mental image is just an optimistic hope of things past. Whatever it is, it would be nice if the two images would be together. Some surprises aren't fun, especially first thing in the morning.

Provers 16:31 "Gray hair is a crown of glory; it is gained in a righteous life."

Isaiah 46:4 "Even to your old age I am he, and to gray hairs I will carry you. I have made, and I will bear; I will carry and will save."

_____

_____

_____

_____

_____

_____

_____

_____

_____

~ 14 ~
Missed Opportunities

How many missed opportunities have there been? How many people slipped past and went unnoticed because they didn't meet my standard? They looked disheveled and not like someone with whom I would have anything in common. The blinders on each side of my head forced me to look straight ahead. Sadly, this is all too comfortable for me. With those I have allowed into my inner circle, I am amazed at the love and similarities we share. What about those who walked outside my narrow sight? The woman hurting from a loss so deep it cuts to her core? Where was I? I have been there, too. So many other connections could have bonded us. I could have been a lifeline to her, and she to me. Open my eyes, Lord, so I might not be blinded and open my heart so I might feel.

John 13:34 "A new commandment I give to you, that you love one another: just as I have loved you, you also are to love one another."

Hebrews 13:16 "Do not neglect to do good and to share what you have, for such sacrifices are pleasing to God."

_____

_____

_____

_____

_____

_____

_____

_____

~ 15 ~
We Are Connected

I sit at the coffee café's window. Cars file by like an assembly line – no model exactly the same. Each nameless vehicle has a nameless individual behind the wheel and is unaware of those around her. For some reason this makes me a bit lonely. I'm not sure why. This is the world I live in and each nameless person lives here, too. We share it and are connected to the race we call human.

John 3:16 "For God so loved the world, that he gave his only Son, that whoever believes in him should not perish but have eternal life."

_____

_____

_____

_____

_____

_____

_____

_____

_____

_____

_____

~ 16 ~
Shards of Life

Shattered pieces lay on the tile floor. I walk around so as not to cut my feet, but the sharp edges are right there. It's such a struggle to go around them and I can't go over them. I will only get hurt again. Maybe if I pick up the shards one piece at a time and glue them back together, my life will be like it used to be. The only difference will be a few cracks.

John 16:33 "I have said these things to you, that in me you may have peace. In the world you will have tribulation. But take heart; I have overcome the world."

Joshua 1:9 "Have I not commanded you? Be strong and courageous. Do not be frightened, and do not be dismayed, for the Lord your God is with you wherever you go."

_____

_____

_____

_____

_____

_____

_____

_____

_____

_____

_____

~ 17 ~
Sitting by the Pool at a Resort

The laughter, bits of conversation left and right, some lay in the sun, and others in the shade. I look at the faces one by one and for a moment I step outside myself and realize everyone has a story. I often wonder how many were abused, cheated on, have an illness or even in the luxury of this place are depressed or lonely. Why it is so hard for me to truly see the hearts of those right next to me. The most probable answer is they don't want me to know. It is their secret, their life and story. Perhaps all I can do is be kind and give a smile to add a theme to their chapter for the moment.

I Thessalonians 5:11 "Therefore encourage one another and build one another up, just as you are doing."

Hebrews 10:24-25 "And let us consider how to stir up one another to love and good works, not neglecting to meet together, as is the habit of some, but encouraging one another, and all the more as you see the Day drawing near."

_____

_____

_____

_____

_____

_____

_____

_____

_____

~ 18 ~
At the Park

There is such joy to be seen in the smile of a small child - the laughter in playing with the simplest object. When did I start to grow older? When did those things lose their luster? Gradually the child-like things I loved to do became old and uninteresting. Yet, as I watch this child play, I realize the child I once was is still there. I feel a yearning to run through the sprinkler and cry out in utter abandonment. I want to walk in the rain, stomp my feet in a puddle and leave the hindrances of the adult life behind. It's time to break out of the safety of my age and act like I feel.

Romans 15:12 "May the God of hope fill you with all joy and peace in believing, so that by the power of the Holy Spirit you may abound in hope."

Isaiah 55:12 "For you shall go out in joy and be led forth in peace; the mountains and the hills before you shall break forth into singing, and all the trees of the field shall clap their hands."

_____

_____

_____

_____

_____

_____

_____

_____

_____

~ 19 ~
The Nightly News

My mind constantly questions the good and evil in this world. I understand original sin, but the extent man will go in his deformed desires will never make sense. Cruelty is beyond my comprehension. My heart is too tender to even think about these things. So, God in his infinite wisdom gave us His Word – Jesus will triumph over the evil one day.

John 10:10 "The thief comes only to steal and kill and destroy. I came that they may have life and have it abundantly."

I John 3:8 "Whoever makes a practice of sinning is of the devil, for the devil has been sinning from the beginning. The reason the Son of God appeared was to destroy the works of the devil."

_____

_____

_____

_____

_____

_____

_____

_____

_____

_____

Thoughts of My Grandmother

The elderly are a group of blessed saints who often get tossed aside. What would it feel like to have lost your loved ones? Everyone is gone. To have to rely on others for the slightest chore you used to be able to handle so effortlessly? To wake up each day with exhausting pain, yet there is no one there to acknowledge it? To be looked at by others as slow, useless or ignorant just because you can't do things as fast as you used to? Yet in your heart, you know you were young once and still are inside. You have so much to give, but who will listen or give you their time. We will all be old or even alone one day. Who will come and sit with us? Take time to listen to the elderly in your life. You may discover a young person inside that will fascinate you. A smile goes a long way to bridge the gap of a few generations. Be respectful—we will all be there all too soon.

Leviticus 19:32 "You shall stand up before the gray head and honor the face of an old man, and you shall fear your God: I am the Lord."

Exodus 20:12 "Honor your father and your mother, that your days may be long in the land that the Lord your God is giving you."

_____

_____

_____

_____

_____

_____

_____

_____

_____

~ 21 ~

A Lost Love

The only people who think there's a time limit for grief have never lost a piece of their heart. No manual. No time frame. No judgement. Grief is as individual as a fingerprint. Do what is right for your soul. Take all the time you need.

Matthew 5:14 "Blessed are those who mourn, for they shall be comforted."

Psalm 34:18 "The Lord is near to the brokenhearted and saves the crushed in spirit."

_____

_____

_____

_____

_____

_____

_____

_____

_____

_____

_____

_____

~ 22 ~
The Chaos in My Head

The wind swirls and turns my thoughts as a reed with no weight to hold it up. The tiny dings of the distant chimes are the only constant. Why won't my thoughts sit or rock comfortably back and forth in peace? What has made them so weak to be tossed at the wind's will? I force my concentration to these wayward thoughts. I attempt to catch one. I snatch at it and draw it to the center. It's loneliness. Why here or why now? I release it to grab another and recognize it immediately—despondency. This is often my mind's favorite. Others fly past that are dark in color—fear and dread. As I push those away and concentrate further. Suddenly, I realize there is one that is not scurrying about, but calm and motionless. As I pull closer the color immerges and it grows more brilliant. It reveals an immaculate hue of red. For as it brightens, the darkness fades away. I feel the chaos recede, the wind dies and there is only this one thought. It's the only concept that can turn the darkness and chaos into light and calm. The color of the cross sprinkled with Christ shed blood sacrificed for me. It conquers all. I rise with the peace and comfort of the soft and gentle breeze of Christ love. My mind is at rest.

I John 1:7 "But if we walk in the light, as he is in the light, we have fellowship with one another, and the blood of Jesus his Son cleanses us from all sin."

Hebrews 9:14 "How much more will the blood of Christ, who through the eternal Spirit offered himself without blemish to God, purify our conscience from dead works to serve the living God."

_____

_____

_____

_____

_____

_____

~ 23 ~
Hurtful Words

Their words could have made my heart soar. Sadly, they cut the artery to my heart. I would give up my soul to the harsh words, but the decision is made—no more—no more will I allow the words to hurt or lessen my resolve to be who I am. Instead, the words will be tossed to the wind and my heart will pump freedom within me.

Psalm 19:14 "Let the words of my mouth and the meditation of my heart be acceptable in your sight, O Lord, my rock and my redeemer."

II Timothy 1:7 "For God gave us a spirit not of fear but of power and love and self-control."

_____

_____

_____

_____

_____

_____

_____

_____

_____

_____

_____

~ 24 ~
An Interesting comment from a Stranger

Do not define who I am by my age or dress size. I am not what I appear on the outside. Do not put me in a box to claw out of, only to measure up to what you think I should be.

Romans 12:2 "Do not be conformed to this world, but be transformed by the renewal of your mind, that by testing you may discern what is the will of God, what is good and acceptable and perfect."

II Corinthians 5:17 "Therefore, if anyone is in Christ, he is a new creation. The old has passed away; behold, the new has come."

_____

_____

_____

_____

_____

_____

_____

_____

_____

_____

_____

~ 25 ~
Precious Moments

Why is it so hard to hold on to the sweet cozy moments of our lives? I sit and cuddle a grandchild and feel the warm blanket of contentment slowly cover me from head to toe. I sit in that same spot later, close my eyes and attempt to relive that precious moment. It eludes me. I realize I can't relive the past—I can only live in the moment.

Ephesians 5:20 "Giving thanks always and for everything to God the Father in the name of our Lord Jesus Christ"

I Thessalonians 5:18 "Give thanks in all circumstances; for this is the will of God in Christ Jesus for you."

_____

_____

_____

_____

_____

_____

_____

_____

_____

_____

_____

~ 26 ~
I Drove Past a Prison

Four walls, an internal clock that won't stop ticking. How did an innocent girl or boy turn into something society deemed necessary to put away? Could this have been prevented? Who are the biological donors to this child's demise? Are they to blame or did nature just reach out and chew up these children earlier that the rest of the world. There are all kinds of prisons. Most are too obvious: cement walls, bars on the doors and windows. But the majority are kept hidden in the hearts that are locked away by hate, bitterness and lack of forgiveness. Although many will be physically put away from society by their behavior, others will keep themselves in their own prison by their stubbornness.

Ephesians 4:32 "Be kind to one another, tenderhearted, forgiving one another, as God in Christ forgave you."

I John 4:20 "If anyone says, "I love God," and hates his brother, he is a liar; for he who does not love his brother whom he has seen cannot love God whom he has not seen."

_____

_____

_____

_____

_____

_____

_____

_____

~ 27 ~
Where Did the Last Ten Years Go?

The time in my life when I don't jump out of bed, but slowly push one foot at a time on the floor and push myself up. I wait patiently for my body to wake up and the muscles to stretch so my movement is somewhat fluid. The "golden years" are not so golden. It is a patient heart that pushes through the myriad of pain which tries to stop my movement and keeps me from living my daily life. The old sayings, "Youth is wasted on the young" has a ring of truth. Yet I would not have the scars seen not only by the naked eye or those not seen which keeps me going to fight this battle with age. The young couldn't handle it.

Galatians 6:9 "And let us not grow weary of doing good, for in due season we will reap, if we do not give up."

I Corinthians 9:24-27 "Do you not know that in a race all the runners run, but only one receives the prize? So run that you may obtain it. Every athlete exercises self-control in all things. They do it to receive a perishable wreath, but we are imperishable. So I do not run aimlessly; I do not box as one beating the air. But I discipline my body and keep it under control, lest after preaching to others I myself should be disqualified."

_____

_____

_____

_____

_____

_____

_____

_____

~ 28 ~
Tomorrow's Road

I am continuing to work on who I am and what my role is. It is all too clear to me and other times I'm just a cloudy mist with no beginning or end. I get confused and don't know which way to turn – yet in my soul I know I need only look up to see God clearly. I'm a prisoner with the jail door wide open, just standing there, with a dumbfounded look on my face. I'm the terminally ill with the cure in my hands and yet I can't seem to get myself to swallow it. God, you are my pardon and my cure. Break the shackles, walk out of the jail, drink the elixir of life and be free to be what I will. I will look at God's creations and take joy: it is for you and me. I will not be afraid to be what I was meant to be. I will take hold of the life offered and be strong in this resolve, for it is as it should be. I am in control of who I am and what I become. I will be kind in this resolve and follow this yellow-brick road.

Psalm 18:2 "The Lord is my rock and my fortress and my deliverer, my God, my rock, in whom I take refuge, my shield, and the horn of my salvation, my stronghold."

Matthew 5:16 "In the same way, let your light shine before others, so that they may see your good works and give glory to your Father who is in heaven."

_____

_____

_____

_____

_____

_____

_____

_____

Time Spent with God

What is the essence of prayer? Is it the words spoken? Do God need to hear them or does he just need the attitude the words bring? Why is it so hard to do or give time to? We talk to others all the time. God deserves all we have.

Ephesians 6:18 "Praying at all times in the Spirit, with all prayer and supplication. To that end keep alert with all perseverance, making supplication for all the saints,"

Romans 8:26 "Likewise the Spirit helps us in our weakness. For we do not know what to pray for as we ought, but the Spirit himself intercedes for us with groanings too deep for words."

_____

_____

_____

_____

_____

_____

_____

_____

_____

_____

_____

~ 30 ~
I Am Me

What is it about new shoes, haircut, ring, anklet, tattoo, or ear ring that makes me feel so good when I go out and get them? Am I so materialistic when it brings such joy? Why can a good hair day or new outfit fill me with a renewed confidence? Is that the world in me? Or do I just enjoy the little things of life which make me uniquely me?

Jeremiah 29:11 "For I know the plans I have for you, declares the LORD, plans for welfare and not for evil, to give you a future and a hope."

_____

_____

_____

_____

_____

_____

_____

_____

_____

_____

_____

Have You Ever Felt a Bit Unworthy? Well Stop It!

Another year passes and my age is +1, but I feel no different than I did 24 hours ago. Nothing has changed, except the warmth of blessings showered on me like a summer rain which trickles down from head to toe. Laughter, jokes, children, grandchildren, loving husband, secure future and health. These blessings of God never expected, but given freely. My first impulse is to think, "I'm not worthy." But this time, I realize I am worthy. I am God's child. He made me and allowed these blessings and they are mine as long as he sees fit. My life started as a canvas ready to be filled with the artist sense of style and color for only me. I am unique and one of a kind in God's gallery.

Psalm 139:14 "I praise you, for I am fearfully and wonderfully made. Wonderful are your works; my soul knows it very well."

Isaiah 40:26 "Lift up your eyes on high and see: who created these? He who brings out their host by number, calling them all by name, by the greatness of his might, and because he is strong in power not one is missing."

_____

_____

_____

_____

_____

_____

_____

_____

_____

~ *About Dianna* ~

Dianna Beamis Good is married with two grown children and four grandchildren. She is a member of the Northern Arizona Word Weavers. Her stories have appeared in Christmas Story Collection, A Time to Blossom, Spoken Moments, Stupid Moments, Chicken Soup for the Soul: Military Families, and Loving Moments.